DRESSING THE BEAR

Dressing the Bear

poems by Susan L. Leary

Winner of the 2023 Louise Bogan Award

TRIO
HOUSE
PRESS

Leary, Susan L.
1st edition

ISBN: 978-1-949487-23-7
Library of Congress Control Number: 2023946396

Interior design by Hadley Hendrix
Cover design by Joel W. Coggins
Editing by Kris Bigalk and Patrick Werle

Trio House Press, Inc.
Minneapolis
www.triohousepress.org

In loving memory

Brian Lee Kilpatrick

12/29/1990 ~ 9/24/2020

Table of Contents

II.

III.

IV.

She had a small gold bird in her pocket he'd given her long ago. They both wanted so much for it to sing.

—Mark Irwin, "A Brief History of Eternity"

The world does keep moving, and it can be a damn cruel place. But those moments of stillness, that place, that's the kingdom of God. And that place will never abandon you.

—Sound of Metal

If, Elsewhere

You startled yourself
with your own death
as I startled myself
with the facts. Nightly,
my dreams of you
have become grotesque.
We stand in the midst
of a war zone
on opposite sides
of a river. I call to you
but you have forgotten
your own name.
When I wake,
I write your epitaph
on my left palm
& imagine peonies
blooming from your chest.
I write the tiniest,
most unambitious poem
to keep you alive,
even if you must be
alive elsewhere.
Believe me,
you have failed
at nothing.
That if you will
allow it, across this rush
of wild water, I will mouth
your name to you.
That you might finally
leave me, Brother, let me
tell you who you are…

I.

Complicity

The palm reader has commenced her weeping,
the lines etched into my brother's skin fleeing
each other at sharp angles. Her attempts to soften
them of their panic with her thumb, a fiasco.
The boy's future avoiding examination like a pair
of striped legs curling back beneath the house
that crushed them.

Have we not all been crushed
by what shelters us?
By a sun hauled from the sky
& collapsed into rubies, my brother
carrying the wreck of it
in his hands.

With soap & water,
I scrub those hands clean.
I do the killing. I do
what it takes to keep a boy
from realizing something
inside him has already died.

All day, my brother sleeping atop a bed of pine
needles & cinderblock, his body refusing itself mercy
by refusing to lie flat against the earth. *Steady now,*
says the palm reader. *Steady now,* says the palm—& maybe
my brother has tried. Maybe I have too, nodding with his trembling
hand in mine each time he says, *I don't care about who
I could be. I only want more of who I am.*

When the Belly of a Thing Is Cut Open,
the World Must Repent of What It's Ravaged

My brother walked through the world with a knife
strapped to his hip. A boy of noble purpose, ready
to stop a bullet or free the rubberbanded stems

of store-bought tulips. Always a reason for him
to lift the loose fabric of his shirt & pull the blade
from its sheath, his hand swiftly cutting bait, stray

threads, or gum from the carpet. As he dug a splinter
from my palm once, I trusted him with the sharpness
because the sharpness made him tender, though

he believed it made him a man. When I say my brother
was in the business of altering the course of things,
I mean wound is another word for amenable,

for progress, for portal. Each December, my brother
sneaking off to the garage to slow-dagger a new hole
into the leather of his belt. At the time, I didn't know

the meaning, but in the autopsy report, his teeth
are described as stained & full of cavities, each life
containing many smaller lives, each one worth noting.

Perhaps why, in the newest dream, my brother curates
a museum of his body, his structures capped in glass
jars & labeled on strips of masking tape with a Sharpie.

He refers to his teeth as *tiny clawfoot tubs*. His liver,
a lifeboat for kings. His nose, *a miniature cello*.
As I walk inside the meat of him, I press my hand

to my cheek & rub the ache. I spit blood into a metal
pail & stop my breath for 60 seconds. I know my brother
suffered, but suffering has nothing to do with wounds.

Rather, wounds have everything to do with the eyes.
As he points to the *pink loofah* that is his spleen,
I wish to look away, but I'm awake now & his body,

a matter of public record, what's left of him weighed
out in grams. The right & left lungs, 810 & 650 grams,
respectively, both distended & full of bronchial foam.

We can stand to learn something from this.
Not the drugs, but the ferocity of life & science,
patience & technique. Under the medical examiner's

lamplight, everyone a tiny shipwreck on icy slab.
As towards the end of the dream, I find my brother
bent over a body, seriously in task, his back to me

& his knife slumbering against his thigh. When
he asks what I take him to be doing, I say dressing
a deer or gutting a fish, to which he tells me, *No.*

The body here is not dead—& like the body before
him, in this life, my brother was wounded enough.
Yet my brother had not been touched, been seen.

Only the Finest Track Stars Smoke Newports

Or so says my brother, all thinned-out muscle & magic trick, sliding onto the back porch with a shit-eating grin, when he halts, a pack of menthols flashed in textbook form. He makes a show of stretching the hamstrings & prepping his glutes, that is, of stretching the ghost of his boyhood into a god. *Only the finest track stars smoke Newports*, he says again. Boy slogan for a boy who believes it & surely this boy can impress, this mischievous boy who spins slogan into prayer, who, for a moment, is a little bit wise. As if for once he were saying, *slow down— look at me.* Look at this boy, pent-up with potential.

Ice

It started snowing inside the jail—a deer sprang
from winter's hip & shed its antlers into the left ventricle
of your heart, the fresh rots fencing plasma
from the thin trails of your body.

Too often something is owed
to the wild, but there are deer antlers in your chest
bearing the days-long scrape of tree bark & for this,
you are lucky. Frozen but lucky. Normally, the skull bits
would have been shredded overnight by sated coyotes
or indiscriminate rodents. Now, a thermal undershirt
costs $9 at the commissary & you are good for it, now
you are a woodsman with a flared nostril & steel limbs
selling deer sheds by the pound. The others forget
you paced the periphery.

Soon, the deer will escape
the body's thickets for a life more spacious than a single
room, for thick velvet curtains, tiny scraps of meat dangling
from the meandering crown, while you remain coatless,
only the satisfaction of knowing what's graced you,
hurt you. You wouldn't wish nature on your cruelest enemy.
I would.

On the outside, deer antlers are often shed
along the forest floor miles apart. We, too, are miles apart.
Yet, I can hear the heavy hoof of your heart beating
beneath the earth, poppies swarming the snow-fire
fields—you, with your arms bent into a makeshift pillow
behind your head, almost warm.

A Man Does His Apologizing out in the Wilderness

But you have no regard for funerals, instead of mercy, extending a glass box in the shape of a keel no bigger than my palm. Inside, a miniature starling swathed in spider silk & stilled to sleep, its iridescent arms spread out from under it. You thrive

in convincing me we are the bird, each of us a wing—our bodies back-to-back in a fetal position & tangled into a single spine, our limbs curling into hydrangeas. It is a curse to be turned to stone, but you are a god exerting the greatest effort to remain idle. You do not notice

the sadness of your wasteful blooms, nor that of the starling, persistent in its slumber until one of us agrees to become the other & I refuse to bend. Why not await the mercy of animation, the earth denied the delicate erosion of your bones, until peering inside the glass, all that's left are feathers.

Even Heaven Requires Your Survival

There are flowers inside other flowers
        & there are drugs inside the flowerpots.

Shame laced inside snowfall & tar. Brother,
        I'm afraid to say you walked out on your life

trying to make a home of it. What fortune, then, to be
        met by the hailing of a new sun & the lesser light

of its aftermath. Even in paradise, there is an aftermath
        & this time, you are to be a better host. How to say it

plainly? What happened to you as a child was not all that
        interesting. Brother, only in a world that takes you hostage,

        are you free.

Misspent & Yet—

Those who love you are your descendants now. With your washed bones, we erect a house at your gravesite & pretend you are quick to forgive. Either our offerings are reckless or time has little intention. Day-old lilacs drown themselves in rainfall while we interrogate the glass. As if there were something to learn, as if we hadn't already put down our tools & failed to love properly. I'd be traumatized if I dug the dog up, you'd once said. The fields are clotted as it is & tenderness is not in the rot. Still, a trail of nerves could lead us anywhere. I keep busy. *We* keep busy. We dress our children in your smoke-filled clothes & dream the empty architecture into a mirror made of sea. Trial & error is overrated & vigilance, often misguided. As now, you are not even here. As before the blaze, in handing the plastic bag to the funeral home director, you'd think it funny we'd forgotten to give you shoes.

Dressing the Bear

for Brittany

This time, we give the body shoes. The body of a bear
my brother is building at a factory in the mall to give
to the girl he's loved since the sixth grade. I'm there to pay
for the bear & to speak of none of it, which is fine
because I'm good at hiding the ways my brother has wanted.
This time is different. At each station, my brother stuffs
only the good parts of himself inside the slack fur.
He gives the bear perfumed bones & shiny gold laces
& breathes so as not to snap them. He considers what the girl
wants & I consider his face as he forgets he has one,
as if in loving the girl & loving her limb by clothed limb,
for once, my brother can love himself. Probably,
that bear is in a Florida landfill, barefoot & decapitated,
its floral button-down shirt torn & full of crawfish stains.
But the girl arrives at my brother's service in a blue & pink
striped dress, a burst skeleton of human sky—& I remember
the air as we exited the mall into the sunset that day, the reddest bomb
of a fist before us. Then my brother, with insight delicate
enough not to wreck the evening: *It's harder to catch*
the sunrise, he says. *You have to really want it.*

I Ask the Antagonist within Me to Bless My Brother, Then I Ask My Brother for a Metaphor

One horse galloping toward another horse, one sword
toward another sword, is not much different
from how he spends his days, stable
as breath, striking blood from the sky, then peeling back
time with his dirty hands. There's a small heaven
that pools inside the bathwater the color
of rust, where despite victory, the horse is denied
its pleasure, the blade dulled by the ragged edge of blossoms
& rock bottom, the most ordinary of days.

So Long Must Love Be in the Overlooking

Or in the hope the son will change.
But from the back window, the jail stands visibly
against the moonlight, as if God created sight
lines only to call a mother's bluff.
Sometimes a mother must go to the police
in good faith. She must go with a compulsion to steal
light from God because doesn't God have enough
light already? What's there for her in this faint glow of stars
or tiny horseshoe of moon? Not even language
beautiful as this can keep her son from dying. Just once,
let there be no more correcting the balance. No overlooking
the crimes. The same will be true of the mother
& the son, even should the boy return home. That is,
sometimes a mother must put her life
on hold. Sometimes forever.

The Professor Asks Me to Write a Joyful Poem

One without drugs or sadness
or mention of your death. One
in which you don't beat your fists
bloody against a palm. I am
disobedient as is joy as is you,
as is the better version of the truth
that lives inside the defense. Is it more
profound to say walking *towards*
or walking *away*? Somehow, with me,
you're always doing both: forgetting
the air mattress & your Greyhound
ticket, then forgetting to breathe.
Is forgetfulness a form of joy
or of disobedience? The day I forgot
the plunger at Ace Hardware
was the day you forgot
to put my car in park. You were fifteen,
so my fault, but as the car rolled
nearer the storefront, we laughed
through the panic because joy is you
is disobedience is me, is the weather
we last looked upon your face.
A shit storm, you'd have said,
as we ran out to the parking lot, pelted
by the sky's sadness & with nothing
for a shield, while I was thinking
how nice it would have been
to spend a day with you in the rain.

Should You Forget Your Way Home, Remember
the World Becomes Clearer the Closer You Hold It to Your Face

In case of an administrative
error, there is a team of ghosts
assembled inside a singe
of angel mane & threaded
through the tiniest needle. Someone
must be accountable for the enormous
migration about to take place. Someone
must prepare a stack
of rags & buckets of ice water.

Forget the hole in the shirt. Once,
you were so determined, you cut
your hands off
at the wrists & starved
yourself to shimmy
through this minor hole
called *life*. Does the splendor
or the scar do the sewing? Brother,
I don't know. But even tender
words are terminal—& inside
the long growl of your grown
man's voice, whenever you said
the word, *button*,
I could almost make you
small again in my mind.

II.

Elegy Downstream

It happened
as Wednesday spilled
into Thursday—somewhat
unscheduled
& somewhat on time.

Clean

I often worried when I got the call, I'd be unprepared.
But the morning my brother dies, all the good clothes
in the house are clean. So I tell myself to get on with it.
& later, standing over my brother, I think whoever
prepared his body must love what they do. Because he looks
so clean. Cleaner, even, than when he'd doze on the couch
midafternoons to Hank Williams or Johnny Cash.
The fatigue of living wiped from his cheeks. & today,
as then, the same stillness stretched across his eyes.
The same tiny shovels for thumbs. & when I find the strength
to rest a hand atop his, I shake him a little to tell him
I wore his favorite dress: summery & sand-colored with splotches
of blue. & while it seems so symbolic, it's all rather simple.
I wear a blue-patterned dress because my brother loved
the ocean. & because my brother was lonely & broken,
he couldn't kick drugs. But I love my brother & the morning
he dies, all the good clothes in the house are clean.
So I tell him: *Clean.*

Were God a Boy or a River Makes No Difference

Every boy is ancient & a river is as much a body
as it is a pair of hands. Who holds the blade that fails

against the rush? What within the boy dissolves every trace
of violence? The river speaks a name & a soft halo of sun

hovers over steel. The sun is gentle on the boy's face.
Which is preferred? That each dawn be new light or the same

light remerged for centuries. Strange metaphor for *a resilient
self*. Even the wind appears reckless in its bloom-scattering

tantrums yet when a boy drowns, we never think to ask
if the river meant to do it. The river is but river stretching

on for miles & the boy returns home a small god walking
through fields. Until, there is no more light. Until, the stakes

of the ritual are so high the river can only mourn itself.
The brain placed back inside the stomach & a pair of new

hands folded over a corpse. How does the boy come to know
himself now? Whose name does he cry out over the wide,

rippling shoulders of the living? Mine, yours, his own,
the troubled sun's—for whom does it even matter?

Death Notice

There is such a thing as the last hurrah, as an unforgivable grammatical mistake.

Time's up! Pencils down! says the proctor.

On the way out, God's shadow lengthening across the school yard by the minute.

Another strange derangement of fact: if lucky,

> your life will be worth the sadness of maybe one or two people.

In the Weeks after My Brother Dies

The way through grief is grieving.
—*Jane Hamilton*

Except I am trying too hard. Is the dead bird trying
too hard to be dead? With concrete for a pillow, he is as eye-
catching & calm as he is grotesque. Still, I forgo feeling
for action. At 4:41PM, I plant three succulents & lather
myself in plumeria-scented body wash. The number 29
appears everywhere. When it rains, I google facts
about turquoise & the reddest sunsets, about dolphins that swim
in the boat's wake. My grief means I must ransack
a life. Daily, I clean your rifle & put your unwashed
shirt in a Ziploc bag. I buy a mug with the letter
'B' & one that says, *May there always be*
an angel by your side. Apparently, I have nothing
in common with myself anymore. When I get the urge
to write, I do not write. Rather, I ask strangers in the produce
section if they believe in life

after death. Most people tend not to answer. I don't
mind. In the evenings, I pour two glasses of the cheapest
Cabernet (neither of which I drink) & map each
detail of the bottle's label with my finger: a dreaming
tree with tiny, gold-foiled leaves & in its shade,
a swath of upturned roots. It's unclear as to whether I fear
or desire your ghost. So much so, I sleep
with the hall light on & I sleep upside down on the bed,
a palmful of blue seashells arranged into a sail
on the nightstand. By midnight, I am counting
ants instead of sheep. *Ninety-eight, ninety-nine, one*
hundred of those pitch-dark pallbearers that know better
than to waste a morsel of bread, a sliver of feather
or blossom—so believe me when I say, I am
desperate. When I say, I too am hungry for God.

Twisted Threads

When we look to God, we mean to look head on
at what's in our peripheral vision, but God is tied
to the periphery by a taut string. As we glance to the right
or left, God moves proportionally out of view.
Why? we ask. The better
question: How did the string
come to be there?

When I dream of my brother, we sit
side-by-side in a 1969 grabber blue Shelby.
We talk normal talk, but my brother refuses
to face me. As I turn towards him, he turns
towards the window. As I turn back
to the dash, so does he. We move
in sync like this for hours.

It is the dreamer
who dreams, but how do those
who visit the dreamer come to be there? How
does God or my brother begin to relax
the string? At some point, I ask
my brother to take me to the hospital
or the morgue. It doesn't matter which.

I can't, he says: *You're driving.*

Poem in Which I Keyword Search 'My Brother'

Give me a map of the world & I can find my brother anywhere. At 63 Brian Avenue in Dublin or in Eden District at Brothers Lake. According to legend, Brothers Lake was named for two brothers who drowned in the water's hands on their way to church. One boy's saving tied to two boys' destruction. Days later, a procession of horses at the water's edge carrying tiny coffins on their backs.

Ask my brother & he'll tell you he was to die young because he, too, was legend. Proud & quiet in his suffering, a thousand empty bottles sunken into the frantic lake of his heart.

& against the enfolding blue, the tragedy at Brothers Lake, was that the fate of the brothers or the fate of the water? A single hand grasping after its double. The last time I held my brother's hands, he'd been in a refrigerator for days. For once, his cold & iron hands, the hands of a king. Hands I held in December as we lowered the ash of his body into the Gulf. Floating yellow blooms the new coordinates of a thing.

& though I am low on faith, if asked where my brother is, I'll tell you now I know. Because just today, I have died there three times already.

Threshold

We were simply
standing
inside the doorway
of my apartment,
the last place
we were each other
before you died.

Constructive Criticism

My mother asks why I must be *the crying,*
left-behind person. Surely, there is something

to be rosy about. Even the dead are rosy with delight.
This is the thing about questions. They pretend

to be curious but mostly they are invested
in change. I should be less sorry someone has died,

less occupied by dreams of a hellish baptism.
Nightly, my grown brother's casket a kiddie pool

filled with boiling water—my brother, a baby again
& drowning. My mother would be pleased.

Each morning, I awaken rosy: my forearms red
& blistered. The blood vessels in my right eye,

burst. My brother left behind in every dream.
My brother, crying.

Grief, without Design—

Weeds are resilient. They grow quite well without any care.

       Everything a body learns, it learns by practice.
       A body learns to grieve because it fails to grieve properly.

What is a weed? A weed is a plant that grows where it is not wanted. It may grow in disturbed areas, such as bare spots in a lawn.

       A body knows itself only when it breaks—when the heart
       is hollowed like a rotting tooth & the stomach split by sky.

Turfgrass and weeds have the same basic requirements: soil nutrients, water, space, and light. These are limited, so turf and weeds are in competition for them.

       When we say a body ages, we mean a body wounds the earth
       & the earth wounds a body back. Sow—

If you can prevent weeds, you will not have to manage them.

       What is labor if not a body bent in prayer?
       What is prayer if not a body bent into its aftermath?

Some weed seeds have hooks or barbs that attach to passing animals. Others have wings that are carried by wind.

       Bone by bone, a body is built to be antagonized by God.
       In each bone, the breath of a boy who was once my brother.

Influencing the Angels

Loss transpires & then comes the recognition you are not God. You are more like the failure of man-made music hovering above an outdoor café. It is your fault you have forgotten how to pray. That you have taken for granted a rare engagement with sky & the imaginary birds that flit behind it, their feathers steeped inside the world like tea. Yet, you're holding the strings. You're holding a penny to the light. Faith, a wooden doll now sitting upon God's lap, the bones of her skull stitched together by horsehair. She preaches to you in absolutes about your beloved. She refrains from using the word *tender* more than twice. Soon, you start believing. Soon it occurs to you, only God cannot tell you what you want to hear.

"Translation, by Hand, across a River"

—Marina Tsvetaeva

I could describe through the medieval fabrics, a stitch
      of light, the box that holds the heavy barrel

of your frame, or the garments your brother picked out. But
      there'd be nothing to debate with a photo. Certain mediums

are more efficient than others: the photographer sets faith
      in his camera, the painter paints, while the poet applies

pressure to the words. & before the blood is suctioned
      from the body, aren't we all condemned to the knees, trying

to say I love you in interminably wrong ways? A translation
      by hand, across a river. They say a photo knows

more about a person than he can know about himself & you've been
      through enough. Which is why I never reach

for my phone. Again, I describe the particulars to you of a room:
      our fluency in direness & apology, the leniency

of rain. Dust asleep on the sill. But the line is the unit of the poem
      & the line ends. We were together. It was Sunday.

You, Brother

When I am not writing a poem, I speak
to my dead brother & consider my audience.

I say, Brother, I am talking to you. I am talking
to you because you assumes I am not alone.

That you see my outstretched hand before you
& put your fingertips to mine. To you, I say things like:

The tomatoes are turning red & the girl in Apt. 6
moved out. & if you hear this, you know I may very well quit

poetry because I have only one poem left. That is, I may
die from this sorrow, from not knowing within the empty

atmosphere of the living room whether or not
you have left. & if I am not speaking to you, perhaps

I am speaking to God. But if there is no God
& no guest, there is no one to witness any of it.

Brother, there is cruelty in that.

Elegy Upstream

The day before
you died,
you'd ordered
a kayak
online. We're still
waiting
for it to arrive.

III.

Heat

My brother is allowed to shower once a day

at the jail & so every morning, a scalding.

I would've thought the opposite. A raw-nerved

shiver. A flood of winter that pinpricks

the bone. *But cold don't leave an imprint,*

my brother says. 60 seconds: wash up,

wash down—heat serving its purpose,

sufficient even to cook up my brother's

Ramen Noodles & instant coffee

from the commissary. Because only he

can know the frank intimidation

of water. The way it turns the skin red

in a blitz & reveals to the self the wound

that is one's body. When I was a baby,

my first word was hot. *Hot, hot,* I'd say,

wobbling around the kitchen, my mouth

as wide as my fingers that stretched

outward towards the stove. How lucky I was

to learn language without reckoning

its meaning. To look up into adult eyes

as translucent & abundant as water,

while my brother, cool-veined & calloused,

learned the instinct that forces the hand away.

(239) 354-7068

This is a pre-paid call from an inmate at the Collier County Jail.
This is a call from *Brian*.
To accept this call, please press zero.
Your current balance is sixteen dollars and eighty-eight cents.
This is a call from a correctional facility and is subject to monitoring and recording.
Thank you for using Global Tel Link.

Well hello, hello.

Undisclosed Archetypal Structure

Let me describe
      the beginning
           & the ending
     to you.
The second son
     is born into a state
        of longing:
           the mirror
       image,
    the life
despaired,
     the mirror
       that is no
          mirror
     at all.
    You see
him clearest
    in the light
      that devours
         the casket
           whole,
       & all
     the longing,
   immediately
is ours.

This is the poem in which the father leaves

In which the commonplace becomes the exponential
and *was* and *is* share the same meaning.

In which, at the kitchen counter, you drop the knife
clean through the dog's skull.

A perfect wound,
neither deliberate nor accidental.

Mortality, Mathematically Speaking & with a Nod to Flavor Flav

Only feigned innocence can be expected.
Those who say *You don't know that?* are precisely those

who should have taught it to you. Time of death minus
time of trauma equals time of burden. Repeat this & no one

will care. The last thing my brother googled was *Tiffany Pollard
and Flavor Flav.* The last thing I googled, *Does it hurt to die*

by overdose? We all remain mentorless, but amidst this human
drama, the dead stay active too. A body asleep still reads

the room. A body asleep is still roiling. How else to keep onward
in this life or thereafter when all we want is love? We wear a clock

around our necks & measure the time in years. $29 - 8 = 21$.
A feat, I'd say. I wish I'd told you sooner.

In the Silhouette of Aftermath, Hindsight Fails
the Search Party, the Mourner

Everything is known as the back of a hand except
for the explanation. My brother is not a poem
& this is not a poem in which the history
is cleared. Often, the afterparty is not much different
from the funeral. Often, the answer to the question is
D) *all of the above.* There's the wovenness
of a thing & then there's the symbol. The gaping
hole in the statue. The mouth unafraid to forger
the heart. There's no difference between the container
& the contained because together they create
the containing. Even dreams require our intelligence
& by morning, who knows what we will remember?
Last night, we were drowning or dancing. We were
trying to spell *brother* without the letter b. Who is *we*?
Who is memory's protagonist when language fails
& succeeds at the task? With grace, my brother held
daylight within the width of his arms & together
we held the non-world between us. Silhouette of a boy
who never needed to explain himself. Don't give me
any credit. We are all obsessed with what happened.
Where were we when it was happening?

Though the Stars Were an Empty Threat, Neither of Us Were Fools

That was the summer I had a bad attitude
& I fought you on every detail.
You insisted Orion had a little dog
in the sky & I insisted the dog
was left-handed. Were we a constellation
of stars, we'd be a set of parallel lines
unworthy of the imagination.
Two hunters with nothing
to hunt, still brandishing their swords
against the wind. We play
a more perfect game. On the company's
organizational chart, we draw a dotted
line to Truth. I pretend, you pretend,
not to know what the other wishes
to conceal. A version of plate tectonics
adapted to human speech
in which masculinity is made
permissible. Here are your choices,
your own voice says. You, alone,
must make them. That was the same summer
we took an IQ test together
over the phone & I read the questions
aloud as you memorized the potential
answers. It was the first time
you were more without a script
than me. Orion, with a chance to lay down
his sword. We tested each other
on what we *knew*, keeping distance
as trees of the same species keep
distance at the crown, oblivious
to the shrewd geometry of our shared life,
that, Brother, from the very beginning,
the love between us was bound up
in all we didn't.

dwelling

again my brother calls in the middle of *Property Brothers*
to tell me he can build a better house. a blue house with a bluer door
& a hundred noiseless windows where i can live overlooking the sea.

a writing desk. sheets of sun stacked to the ceiling like paper. miniature
rooms hidden inside every doorknob, one with a library the size
of my thumb, fleabane vased in barnacles.

i could live there, i say. in the house built in the company of tv static
& other troubled men. feces on the walls & pillows soaked in piss,
jumpsuit removed & toothpaste spread over one man's genitals.

yes, even there, my brother thought beauty. even there, resting
besides a hemingway novel on the bookshelf, will be an immaculate
little dwelling for his urn.

Blessing

It was the first time
my brother cared for a thing

without having to call it
his own. That was twenty years ago.

Even the January sun
was drenched in honey that day

& I have known love
but a few times.

Against the reigning blue,
we spoke a private, muted language.

In the dead of my hands,
I still carry my brother's heartbeat

through the light.

Today

You smell of Arm & Hammer.

I button your shirts onto the hanger,

round your socks,

patch the holes in your body with dryer sheets.

Oracle

I dreamt the evening
saved me, but my brother

saved me,
when I thought

I saw him
over another man's

shoulder, I did,
boy prophet

wearing a crown
of cream roses

& chewing
on Nicorette gum,

his eyes
echoing his voice

as he softened
the lines

of my palms
into his fingertips

the night before,
saying,

*Trust me, it will be
better this way.*

The Dead Need	Answers Also
The grief counselor asks	me to imagine
you in the chair	across from me.
A wooden chair	in a sequined slat of light
& noisy as an attic.	I can't beat it,
you say, though	Brother, neither can I.
& that I am	*here*
& you	*there*
makes me	no better.

Poem Beginning with Two Lines from William Carlos Williams

So much depends
upon

the straw
wrapper from *Sonic*

stuffed inside
your fishing pack,

upon the glow
& rattle

of the bathroom
lights,

the color of
heroin,

lovely as snow
or a finger's

pinch
of the earth.

& your last
words,

so much depends
upon

your last
words, six hours

earlier,
that convinced

nobody
of nothing—

I'm not gonna die.
I'm goin' out in a blaze of glory!

Mugshot

Racked by the idea of uselessness, we pass a small riot
through a gap in our teeth, the city noticeably at risk
of what's wild in us. In every case of its use,
actually is a self-deceiving word.

The windows we peer out of are coy today & the spiders,
asleep in the eye sockets. What we give over to madness?
What we sacrifice to create conditions that might
afford us grace? Our hair suffers the wind

as our throat suffers the queen. The roof, the implacable
jumper. Lucky for us, it takes a combined effort to dispose
of a body, more than one limousine driver
to get us where we're going.

Muted sounds break through skin, break through lilacs,
break through the lid of a wicker casket opening
into the earth, my brother's temper tied
behind his back with willow.

We'd all be better off if we stopped trying to invent what's
possible. On the internet, all that's left of my brother,
an obituary & a mugshot, which means I'm
guilty, never actually prepared to heal.

IV.

Because I Want a Calm to Reiterate

I prefer the first blossom, the first metaphor.
The one in which death is a mother, in which you return
to sleep as once you slept inside the womb, the body
from which you've grown estranged grown again
as yours.

There is mercy in the preparations, every son
scattering a breathful of seeds across the hollow
from which he'd first sprung. Should he die too swiftly,
too soon before the woman who raised him, both would survive it.
In the night-morning of September, a woman may rouse
to the smell of smoke & her son may not rouse at all.

But, O, there is mercy in the preparations. Brother, this time,
too, your mother arrived at the site of you with rain.
She arrived at the sight of you with blossoms.

Cholesteatoma

My brother was born with a tumor
wrapped around the bones
in his right ear. The tiny structure
a snail's shell, this time with the snail
inside. As he gets older, the tumor
puts pressure on the bones & they
break into a shrunken tuba
or finch's claw, something to move
across the board in a child's game.

While the bones get rebuilt,
my brother's hearing is never
the same, which means he has a good
ear & a bad ear—& by the time
he's eleven, a mouth as crude
as The Dude in *The Big Lebowski*. So
it becomes a thing: in the backseat
of the car, my brother leaning to whisper
all the cuss words & dirty jokes
to try & get me to laugh. Which I do,
before murmuring back in his bad
ear words tireless enough to wait.
Because when dying, hearing
is the last sense to go—& as my brother
sank onto the bathroom tile, his head
propped against the tub, perhaps
he heard for the first time
what I'd told him then:

I like you a lot, you know...

These Days

I trade a sack of sugar for a sack of rotting teeth, the great epic for a tale of Time riding to the amusement park in an ambulance. The best wind is carousel wind. The best child, the one who remembers to bring the horses flowers. The joy I don't want is the joy I do.

Calliope music at breakfast time, little cakes strung from the ceiling. Sometimes, I pretend to dance with you by holding your invisible arms in the air. A train whines happily in the far-off like tea. I was to arrive late to your wedding & eat what you served. Now, I gorge my own hands.

Night Train Home with a Famous Poet

for Jarrett Moseley

Or so I think—I've been wrong before about famous people.
But beside me, his face stares down evening with the expectancy
of a coin toss. A poet who goes on his nerve & whose words
fizz with the wholesome drama of seltzer water. Only poet
who can rinse every glass & tell me about the day Lady died.
His poems mean in ways I mean to be: the last ice cube in the ice tray.
April's calm. A sadness as soft as chin hair. & were I to turn
in his direction & mouth that someone I loved very recently died,
the famous poet would reach for my hand & with the tenderest
language tell me my brother loved me.

Last Reverie, with Imperative

Waiting is what's been asked of me. The last student

has exited the classroom & the construction outside has stopped.

The clanging of the metal has stopped & the dust has been blown back

to the earth. There's a holiness to the end of day that feels like waning

light looking back at me—& as I relax into the swivel of my chair,

for a hair of a second, I believe were it quiet enough, the dead

would be smacked awake. & from the sheer splendor of it,

when I tell you to walk through the door, you do.

Si Je Puis

if I can

Then why the moon?

I don't know.

But each brother wanted to be more
like the other brother—   & life

is like a face.

We love the one looking back at us,
we need not see our own.

Floating Gospel

Nothing about the water is heroic. & not because the water is the site of your burial. But because to believe in water is an extraordinary act of faith.

The old man & his marlin leave a trail of blood & bones, a floating gospel which says the beauty of life is that it quiets our fate & love is the very first act.

You love me because I married the boy who first held you, who at the age of six shrouded your body in sailcloth & cradled it into the boat of his own.

When you say I must carry on our name, I take this to mean I should live long enough to return your brother to you.

That as the old bones fragile themselves into dust, into ocean, into bloom, the water will become water again.

We'll Take the Riddle, So Long as It Remains Unanswered

Sometimes the blue is so blue it is every shade of blue at once. The first sound, the back & forth of the blue water. A pair of scissors is blue as is the hem of the blue hand that holds them. The first urge, to snip the blue heron from a swath of nocturnal shoreline. Discernment risks injury, so we sleep inside the blueish swirls of our own blueish bodies, mistake the brute flap of a wing for touch, suffering for the brief amnesia of stars. Distant or beloved, a man's cigar smoke is blue, a vast graffiti of legs stretched into the blue of a borrowed beach chaise, the marooned bones fooled into a comfortable shipwreck, the lungs into ether or sea. A ghost can whet the blade & sit inside the blue of a palm without our knowing. What comes is the world before it'd begun, before the blue was anything other than blue.

The Not-Yet Flowers

You were you until
you named me,
until you cut a path
through the sun
& sought a second
person inside
the oblivion. We are
the ghost & the thing
itself. The body
inside the body,
a collection of feathers
crowded by wings.
With your hand, I draw
myself as a frozen
lake, then the water
moving: your ear
in the shape of my ear.

There is no explanation
for how we speak
to one another.
An assemblage
of sky, the night
is incapable of evading
the night. A wild
horse, no different
from a horse
that's been tamed.
Roiling to slow
their appearance,
the not-yet flowers
are in need of counsel.
The world becoming
the world. The conversation,
not quite over.

You are you & I
am hardly myself.

Not All Kindnesses Are Futile

Which is the opposite of saying people are proof
of God, but on Tuesday, a bird arrives in the shape of a girl
behind a desk & her hands clutch only what's gentle.

I learn she loves a boy who died on the day as you & suddenly,
I'm pulling myself back into the boat, convinced the dead
go somewhere to die. & if not to die, to host elaborate

parties, where without paper & pen, they hatch unlikely
schemes for their grievers. During class discussion, the girl
imbues every sentence with *if you want*. If you want,

you could analyze the difference between grief & longing.
You could analyze the senses, if you want. & delicately,
as you packed another bag, Brother, why leave? You

could get sober, if you want. I understand, now, the slap
of those words, as on this lateral of sky, everyone is
erupting with wisdom & to cope, I assign you new tasks.

Insist the angels quit slacking on pudding. Let the rain
untether itself of ashes. You can allow her in my life forever,
if you want. If you want, her name is Daphne.

Roll Call

By now, the children have fled the schoolyard
& the river has split itself in half. I should have told

you when the last wildflower relinquished its head
to the current, but you were ambitious then & dressed

yourself in sky & paper. Today, there is neither
thread nor rain. Today, the house is vacant

& your pencil dulled to a pinprick. How misbehaved
of me to wait an entire year for the same day

to return, for the same body to appear at the cleft
in the river when the river is becoming wiser. & though

I fail to change alongside you, Brother, I see
the quilted knapsacks of light emptying atop the river

into capable likenesses of your face. The water,
at once, a desk, a suture, & a sieve. Because this poem

is a house & there are children here, at least, I call
them children because, somewhere, a river keeps

on living. Somewhere, you're reciting the alphabet
in your new summer clothes & I am one or two people.

Go now. You are the river in need of a new name.

The Birds, They Too, Are Clean

I take it back—the last line of the last poem, the *go*
now. I agree to quit my want of spectral grace & trouble
with your death no more. Now I am busy being alive,
busy bending my brain towards the mercy in the obstacle.

9 times out of 10, it's the sun that affects the job more
than rain. Here I am absorbing the blow of a new season,
kindling the light. You think I don't notice, but I see you
planted at the foot of my bed shaking your head at me,
at all my handwritten notes in which I try to explain things,

in which I loosen the sky from the river & the river
from the drought, the sparrow from its filthy wings.
& though the absence of explanation decelerates time,
just yesterday buying a pound of fish, I tell your brother
the last line is looming, that it's drifting steadily towards
my mouth, tied to a balloon-less string.

Yet, you'll never leave me, he says, it never ends.
The birds are washing their feathers with the water from our eyes.

Afterglow

There is no more burning,

       just water

             just river

just light.

Notes

The italicized text in "Grief, without Design—" is taken from *Ornamental and Turfgrass Pest Management* (Frederick M. Fishel, University of Florida, Institute of Food and Agricultural Sciences, 2nd edition, 2013).

"Night Train Home with a Famous Poet" references Frank O'Hara's "The Day Lady Died" and Marie Howe's "The Gate."

Acknowledgments

Deepest gratitude is owed to the editors of the publications in which these poems first appeared, at times in altered versions:

A-Minor Magazine:	"You, Brother"
Birdcoat Quarterly:	"Roll Call"; "Though the Stars Were an Empty Threat, Neither of Us Were Fools"
Cathexis Northwest Press:	"Clean"
Crab Creek Review:	"Translation, by Hand, across a River"
DMQ Review:	"These Days"
Gone Lawn:	"Mugshot" *Nominated for the *Best of the Net* Anthology
Eastern Iowa Review:	"Floating Gospel"
The Heartland Review:	"The Birds, They Too, Are Clean"; "Misspent & Yet—" *Finalist for the Joy Bale Boone Poetry Prize
Jet Fuel Review:	"Constructive Criticism"
jmww:	"I Ask the Antagonist within Me to Bless My Brother, Then I Ask My Brother for a Metaphor"
The Journal of Compressed Creative Arts:	"We'll Take the Riddle, So Long as It Remains Unanswered"
The MacGuffin:	"Grief, without Design—"
Mudfish:	"When the Belly of a Thing Is Cut Open, the World Must Repent of What It's Ravaged" *Finalist for the Mudfish Poetry Prize

Parentheses Journal:	"Were God a Boy or a River Makes No Difference" *Nominated for the Pushcart Prize
Pithead Chapel:	"Only the Finest Track Stars Smoke Newports"; "Poem in Which I Keyword Search 'My Brother'"; "Twisted Threads"
Rust + Moth:	"The Professor Asks Me to Write a Joyful Poem"
San Pedro River Review:	"If, Elsewhere"
Soundings East:	"In the Weeks after My Brother Dies"
Spry Literary Journal:	"Complicity"
Superstition Review:	"A Man Does His Apologizing out in the Wilderness"; "Ice"; "Influencing the Angels"; "Should You Forget Your Way Home, Remember the World Becomes Clearer the Closer You Hold It To Your Face"
Tar River Poetry:	"So Long Must Love Be in the Overlooking"
Up the Staircase Quarterly:	"Dressing the Bear"
Unbroken Journal:	"Cholesteatoma"
The West Review:	"Heat"

"Even Heaven Requires Your Survival" first appeared in the anthology, *The Book of Life after Death: Essays & Poems*, with Tolsun Books.

"Because I Want a Calm to Reiterate" first appeared in the anthology, *Bodies: A Preservation of Land & Self*, a project of *Beaver Magazine*.

"This is the poem in which the father leaves" was a Finalist in *Midway Journal*'s -1000 Below: Flash Prose and Poetry Contest.

Thank You

This book would not be possible without the love and support of so many people.

Thank you to my husband, Sean, and to my parents, Karyl and Mike.

Thank you to Trio House Press for making this book a reality, to Kimberly Blaeser for choosing it, and to Jessica Cuello and Matt Rasmussen for lending their words.

Thank you to my MFA cohort—Jarrett Moseley, Carolene Kurien, and Christell Victoria Roach—for offering feedback on many of these poems, for accepting my brother through them, and for friendship.

Thank you to Nathalie Handal for the encouragement.

Thank you to my friends in the writing community, many of whom I've never met in person, but who have read and championed my work from afar and have made me feel loved.

To the students at the University of Miami, thank you.

And to my brother, Brian. I miss you. Hear me talking to you now.

About the Author

Susan L. Leary is the author of three previous poetry collections: *A Buffet Table Fit for Queens* (Small Harbor Publishing, 2023), winner of the Washburn Prize; *Contraband Paradise* (Main Street Rag, 2021); and *This Girl, Your Disciple* (Finishing Line Press, 2019), finalist for The Heartland Review Press Chapbook Prize and semifinalist for the Elyse Wolf Prize. Her poetry and nonfiction have appeared or are forthcoming in such places as *Indiana Review, Tar River Poetry, Superstition Review, The Arkansas International, On the Seawall, Tahoma Literary Review, Cherry Tree*, and *Pithead Chapel*. She has been nominated for both the Pushcart Prize and *Best of the Net* anthologies, and recently she was a finalist for the Mudfish Poetry Prize; a finalist for the Joy Bale Boone Poetry Prize; a finalist for *Midway Journal*'s -1000 Below: Flash Prose and Poetry Contest; and shortlisted for the Arthur Smith Poetry Prize. She holds a B.A., M.A., and M.F.A. from the University of Miami and lives in Indianapolis, IN.

About the Book

Dressing the Bear was designed at Trio House Press through the collaboration of:

Kris Bigalk and Patrick Werle, Editors
Joel W. Coggins, Cover Design
Hadley Hendrix, Interior Design

The text is set in Adobe Caslon Pro.

About the Press

Trio House Press is an independent literary press dedicated to discovering, publishing, and promoting books that enhance culture and the human experience. Trio House Press adheres to and supports all ethical standards and guidelines outlined by the CLMP. For further information, or to consider making a donation to Trio House Press, visit us online at triohousepress.org.

Printed in the USA
CPSIA information can be obtained
at www.ICGtesting.com
LVHW042009030624
782151LV00001B/2